TEST

"One of Dr. Chambers' strengths is his focus on the power of love and forgiveness that creates genuine healing and transformation. Absent, thankfully, a crusade mentality, his approach is steeped in teaching that guides and nurtures our soul-filled human needs and development."

Dr. Steve Van Bockern
Professor Augustana University

"I have known JC Chambers for nearly 40 years and watched him develop his professional life. He is motivated by deep values of compassion and caring based on firm philosophical principles. His personal motivation comes from his faith and supports his clients in their lives, choices, and healing. I have full confidence in him as a professional."

The Reverend Canon Dr. Martin Brokenleg
Retired professor and psychologist

"Dr. JC Chambers is a man of substance. He is true to his calling in both his faith and his profession. He is a student first and his ongoing quest for knowledge and understanding allows him to counsel young people and families through their troubled times in the most skillful and spiritual manner. JC has the compassion, commitment, and courage to provide high-quality mental health services on a strong foundation of faith in God."

Mark Freado
Director, International Training Network
CF Learning

"Dr. Chambers has a unique anointing as a Christian clinician. He knows how to effectively convey the heart of God in a manner that is practical to those who are on their journey of healing through Christ. His unconditional love toward others and his humility make him a mighty tool in the hand of God."

Dr. Raquel Hatter
Commissioner of Human Services, Tennessee

"Dr. Chambers is one of the most effective and realistic therapists I know. I can recommend him with the comfort of knowing the referred clients will be pleased with their choice."

Dr. Nicholas J. Long
President of the Life Space Crisis Intervention Institute

HOPE WITHOUT HYPE, GUIDANCE WITHOUT JUDGMENT

THE STRONGHOLD DIFFERENCE

DR. JC CHAMBERS

THE STRONGHOLD DIFFERENCE

DR. JC CHAMBERS

Dr. Chambers is one of the most effective and realistic therapists I know.

Dr. Nicholas J. Long
President of the Life Space Crisis Intervention Institute

THRONE
PUBLISHING GROUP

Cover design by Jim Hughes

Throne Publishing Group
2329 N Career Ave #215
Sioux Falls, SD 57107
ThronePG.com

TABLE OF CONTENTS

FOREWORD

I have known JC Chambers for many years and have always had great admiration for him. His unique blend of academic rigor, giftedness in facilitating groups, and spiritual depth have made him an enormous gift both to me and to our staff whenever he has come to do training with us.

Dr. Chambers has an uncanny ability to glean the best from a wide variety of models and to synthesize it with laser-like focus to a very challenging population. Stronghold's target audience represents the collision of two very vulnerable populations: adolescents and addicts. It's a segment of society that has caused most in the helping professions to say, "No, thank you, that's not our specialty."

Add to that the challenge of someone being sent to a "therapist" (*Is there a worse title one could possess in the mind of a troubled teenager?*) while still residing in the community that contributed to the addiction. It's no wonder the results of working with this population have been so dismal. Yet it is here that Stronghold's unique blend of clinical excellence and grace-filled methodology has been so effective.

Stronghold comes out of JC Chambers' personal story of growing up in a challenging urban neighborhood, being raised by a loving grandmother, and then moving from the hood to a predominantly white, small Christian college. One can only imagine the challenges that brought on. Grace is formed in fire. It has also afforded JC a level of cross-cultural competence that few who work with our most vulnerable, and largely non-white populations possess.

The world is not short on gifted people. What is more unusual is to see those gifts harnessed in an organizational context. And rarer still, to see them put into a model that can be replicated across other organizations. That, I believe, is the Stronghold Difference.

Dr. Scott Larson

August 5, 2016

Worcester, Massachusetts

INTRODUCTION

What's the difference? We all grapple with this question every day. We may not realize it, but we are constantly in the process of deciding, deciphering, weighing, and making judgments about everything life throws our way. *What difference will it make* if I wake up an hour earlier tomorrow and exercise before work? *What difference will it make* if I have another drink at the bar? *What difference will it make* if I confront my friend about her addiction? Life is challenging. We all have lots of choices to make.

Sometimes life is so challenging that we are tempted to give up answering this question. When we feel weighed down or overwhelmed by the cares of each day, we can lose our ambition to find the difference, to make the best of our lives. Many of the clients I see at my counseling center come to me because they have lost hope. Ultimately, they can't see what difference their own lives make anymore. Perhaps you feel this way. Or maybe you just feel bogged down by anxiety, shame, or addiction. Do you ever wonder what difference it would make if you could be free from those burdens?

The mission of Stronghold is to dispense God's grace to those who need hope again by providing services that are clinically astute, sound, and at the highest level of excellence. Stronghold is *not* in the business of preaching, judging, or proselytizing. Stronghold is about healing. We believe our passion for grace *and* clinical excellence makes all the difference in our offices and in the lives of our clients. This is the Stronghold Difference.

This book is a chance for you to see the transformative power of grace—and to learn what difference love and mercy make in the counseling office. You will hear stories of real people who came to me from broken backgrounds but found new revitalizing hope through grace. You will hear my story: how God snatched me from the jaws of death and put me in a safe place to start Stronghold. You will learn what our offices, convictions, and therapists are all about. We want to offer you an inside look at our day-to-day rhythms and practices. Maybe you will find Stronghold is even a place you want to be.

Most of all, though, I hope this book will prove to you just how much God cares about *you*. At Stronghold, we strive to embody the love, grace, and mercy of Jesus. But we fail sometimes. God, however, does not. Even as you read the following chapters, I pray that God will give you a genuine experience of the love that He has shown us through His son Jesus.

PART ONE

THE STRONGHOLD STORY

CHAPTER ONE

AN INVITATION TO GRACE

Each of us has a unique story. No matter who you are or where you sit as you read this, I'm sure you can recall times of blessings and of trials from your past—both joys and sorrows. This is simply life as we know it, isn't it? The story behind this book began with a simple question I asked myself years ago: Can God use a guy like me to help people experience His loving grace? Years of hardship followed that question— but also seasons of extraordinary grace, love, and mercy from God and others. Through it all I discovered that such seasons are possible. More importantly, though, I learned that there's a place called grace that has the power to heal and transform lives in surprising ways—even in this hurting world. This is the story of Stronghold.

In 1985, I finished up seminary and wondered, *Is Stronghold going to be a group home in Colorado Springs or will it be a counseling center run by me?* I wasn't sure, and something held me back from diving in headfirst—something I now know was terror. I feared the unknown challenges either endeavor would bring. I feared the whole thing might be impossible. Unsure of how to move forward with it, I put Stronghold on the back burner for a few more years.

In September 1993, I became very sick with asthma—status asthmaticus—the most severe form of asthma attacks. My sickness was so severe that I spent more than ten days between the hospital and the ICU. I remember waking up in horrible condition, intubated, and struggling against the asthma. And despite their best efforts and the medication they gave me, the doctors were also struggling to fight my attack. I had never been sick like this in my life. It was a shocking, surreal time.

At several points I thought I was going to die. In fact, the situation became so dire that I welcomed death. I figured it was just my time to go. When the doctors decided to intubate me, I recall telling my wife to prepare for my funeral. I didn't want them sticking my body full of tubes to keep me alive. I would rather die than live hospitalized, intubated, and unable to breathe or live life on my terms.

But God had a different plan. As I went under to be intubated, I heard a voice beckon, "Jamie." Now, I do not regularly hear God speaking to me, but I recognized who was calling to me. I was shocked! No one ever calls me Jamie. Few even know it's my real name. As I slipped into unconsciousness, the voice spoke again: "Jamie, my name is Strong Tower. Come find rest." At the time, the only Bible verse I remember having memorized was Proverbs 18:10, which says, "The name of the Lord is a strong tower; the righteous man runs into it and is safe." When I woke up again I knew instantly that God had something else in store for me. Even though I was still paralyzed, He wasn't going to let me die.

Once my body began to heal and I left the hospital, I started to see how God graciously used this experience to open my eyes to His work in my life. I was able to confront the fears that kept me from considering starting the counseling center. Now, with a fresh perspective and a renewed sense of direction, I set out to start it with the help of friends and partners. This time, I knew exactly what Stronghold would be. It would be a grace-filled counseling center, a place that helped people understand that they mattered to God—that their pain and struggles mattered to Him.

But I couldn't start it; I was too frightened and had been readmitted to the hospital. So a dear colleague and founding partner came to me in need of an opportunity to work and wondered if I would allow her to start Stronghold, as she had clients and required a home base from which to work. From my hospital room we cut the deal, and Stronghold Counseling

Center came to be; on September 15, 1993, it was opened. We are forever grateful to her—she had the guts, or desperation, to take the first step, and frankly, I was still stalling for fear's sake.

Despite all this, I continued to doubt and fear how and when I was to join the practice. I felt insecure and anxious about what God was doing. So, one Wednesday morning I decided to put God to the test. "Here's the deal," I prayed to Him. "If you *really* want me to do this, make three different people approach me today and use the word 'stronghold' in a sentence by eight o'clock tonight." Of course, "stronghold" is a strange word to use in any casual conversation, so I knew the chances were slim.

I was wrong. Once again, God proved to me that He had better plans for my life and for Stronghold. By six o'clock that evening I had heard three different people use "stronghold" in their conversations with me. I absolutely could not believe it. The moment the third individual wrote it after a group therapy meeting that evening, I sprang out of my chair, left the room, and went to wash my hands. My co-therapist was stunned and confused at my news of resigning, but I couldn't stay. It was clear to me that God was up to something. He continued to show me that I wasn't stepping out on a limb. I was walking onto a bridge that He had prepared for me—one that many people had been praying for. I knew I had to join the practice sooner than I had planned.

God's grace, love, and mercy were ultimately what started Stronghold. Through all these events and more, as well as through my fears, He loved me until I was able to trust and follow Him into this work. That's why Stronghold exists: to dispense grace, love, and mercy to its clients. During my early years in seminary, a woman once told me, "What you think is impossible, God will show you is possible." I believe she was right. Not only that, but as you will learn throughout this book, I have experienced that. At Stronghold we want to help people see that what seems impossible to them—health, sanity, stability—is possible with God. We strive to be a grace-based practice because God is grace based with each of us. But what does it mean to be grace based?

GRACE BASED

A grace-based practice is where broken people can experience God as a king who is on their side. It's where they can meet Him *not* as a harsh judge but as a judge who's also a great defense attorney—one who understands His clients and never breaks His promises. At *our* best, you and I are promise breakers. We fail to stay true. But God always comes through. He never lies or goes back on His word. Ever.

This is what Christians call the *New Covenant*. In Scripture, we read that God sent His son Jesus into the world to repair the fractured relationship between Himself and us, humans. This new relationship is based totally on God's love for us and His grace to us. When we look at Jesus, we see God shouting, "I am committed to you. I know you're a knucklehead but I still love you. I am not mad at you."

Grace also means that we can come before God's throne—even in our brokenness—and know with confidence that He won't push us away. This means that people who are grace based can have genuine hope in the face of tragedy because they know God will always meet their ultimate needs. He has promised to! You may be grumbling and hurting, but you can still have hope if you receive God's grace. Jesus said, "I am with you always, to the very end of the age" (Matthew 28:20). He promises to always be there. Stronghold is committed to grace-based counseling because God is so committed to all of us knuckleheads. And just as God commits Himself to us before He corrects us, we promise to commit to our clients even before we try to change them.

SAFETY, CONSISTENCE, AND ACCEPTANCE

We want all our clients to expect three important things from Stronghold: *safety, consistency, and acceptance.* As a grace-based practice, we want everyone to feel safe the moment they step in our doors—safe to be honest with us and with themselves. Secondly, we strive to be consistent with our clients. This takes on various forms. For instance, I always sit in the same chair in my office, and I often say the same things to clients again and again—even if they want to hear something different. I try to be as consistent as possible. Familiarity can be a great comfort, can't it?

Lastly, Stronghold always aims for acceptance. No one is too messed up or broken down to have a place in our office. This is always true, whether you are a prospective client or you have been coming to Stronghold for five years. We refuse to be judgmental because we believe grace is far more transformative in clients' lives, just as it has been in ours. Our goal is to build healthy trust, not to judge our clients. Safety, consistency, and acceptance are the soils in which we plant the seeds of love, grace, and mercy. With God's help, those seeds can grow into beautiful things.

SALLY'S STORY

One of the first substance abuse clients I ever worked with was named Sally. At the time, Sally spent most of her days drunk. Often times she wouldn't even come barging into my office unless she was buzzed! It took her a while, but one day,

Sally finally took my advice to go to Keystone, a treatment center in Sioux Falls. A couple of days after I dropped her off there, Sally called me, complaining that they had taken her anxiety pills and alcohol away. "I didn't know they would do that!" she grumbled. She also informed me of a new discovery: Sally was bipolar.

While Sally's time at Keystone was anything but easy, she made it through treatment and found herself back in my office months later. Now, Sally is sober and refuses to fill her body with unhealthy medication. She even began to pursue reconciliation and healing with her family.

However, Sally still struggles. She tells me how she wakes up to a different battle each morning, unsure of how she will feel or think. Grace has the power to transform lives—as it did Sally's—but by no means does it purge us of all our problems. For Sally, grace gave her the hope that all her problems would pass *eventually*, but not instantly. This was more than enough hope to lead her out of addiction. Sally understands grace.

Our passion is for people like Sally. We know that there are *many* others out there with heavy hearts and noisy heads. (Or both!) We want those people to know there is a safe place they can go to find rest for their souls. We do not want to burden our clients; we want to share the load they are carrying, even if it's crazy, dark, or demonic.

Maybe you feel burdened by something too heavy to carry alone. Maybe someone you know is lost in a daze or addiction. We want you to know that Stronghold is here for you. Our encouragement is this: No matter who you are or what you have done, there is a place for you in God's flock. He does not promise to take away all your struggles now, but He will shepherd you with loving arms and bless you with real soul-satisfying rest. This is what fuels our work at Stronghold each day.

CHAPTER TWO

CLINICAL EXCELLENCE AND GOD'S GRACE

My hope is that chapter one painted a clear picture of what a grace-based practice looks like. But more importantly, I hope that it is a picture of a place you actually *want* to be, an attractive picture to you. This chapter will focus on how grace relates to Stronghold's second characteristic: clinical excellence. For me, clinical excellence has four parts: skill, knowledge, spiritual foundation, and authenticity. These components are the building blocks for Stronghold's passion for excellent grace-based service.

SKILL

If you want to be excellent at anything, you need skills. Accountants need to be quick with numbers; basketball players need to be quick on their feet; artists need skills of patience and creativity. At Stronghold, we look at skill as a utility belt. When you're wearing it, you have instant access to a wide range of tools: a hammer, a tape measure, a level, etc. With these tools, you can accomplish about any task you want. But without them, you're out of luck. Like tools, the right skills at hand allow you to navigate various situations successfully—even when those situations are outside of your comfort zone.

I am naturally introverted. This does not mean that I am afraid of conflict, but it does mean I don't particularly love surprises. Working in counseling over the years has helped me gain conflict-management skills that allow me to confront surprises from which I naturally want to withdraw. Skills help me shift gears and provide care in a myriad of ways. They enable me to be more versatile. Especially as a leader, I have had to acquire skills that allow me to stand in the gap of conflict—even though my temperament isn't wired that way.

KNOWLEDGE

The second part of clinical excellence is knowledge. At Stronghold, we understand knowledge as a multifaceted diamond. Rarely is there one simple answer to the complex questions or problems clients bring to me. Like a diamond, every person is unique, with many different sides.

Because of this, we try to avoid oversimplified solutions for our clients. Instead, we have developed a holistic pool of knowledge that helps us best address our clients' issues. Practically speaking, this means we recognize that things as simple as environmental allergies can cause psychological abnormalities in clients. This isn't a spiritual solution; it's physical. We understand the relationships between physical, spiritual, and emotional health.

On the other hand, knowledge at Stronghold also means we understand what is *not* physiologically oriented. Problems can be medical, moral, or spiritual in nature. It takes knowledge to distinguish a person who is mean from a person who is evil. Not all mean people are evil, and not all evil people are outright mean. Frequently, evil people appear nice and put together—but they are cold and flat on the inside. A one-sided approach to knowledge won't do here. Clinical excellence is knowledge and wisdom that can explore *all* the facets of the diamond, not just the ones in front.

SPIRITUAL FOUNDATION

At Stronghold we have a New Covenant understanding of Christianity. As I explained in chapter one, this means we believe God is our loving Shepherd who has drawn us into

His flock by the life, death, and resurrection of Jesus. He is not harsh with His flock. He guides and instructs us with grace, love, and mercy. So, all the team members at Stronghold strive to treat clients and each other in Christlike ways. Sometimes it's messy because we're imperfect—but He understands.

A spiritual foundation is a vital part of clinical excellence because it keeps us from having a superior attitude toward anyone. But sometimes I have to remind my team (and myself) that we must not have a one-up-one-down posture. It is easy to slide into a prideful, judgmental state in our competitive world. But God's grace keeps us humble and honest with one another and with clients. This goes beyond being clinically sound. It's a heart thing.

AUTHENTICITY

The fourth and final component of clinical excellence at Stronghold is authenticity. Authenticity is the ability to own your mistakes when you make them and to know your talents and gifts—and own them too! It is a sense of honesty and transparency with yourself and with clients. Authenticity protects against pretending and hypocrisy. On the other hand, it frees us to see and accept what we're genuinely good at.

I never want my employees or partners at Stronghold pretending like they aren't gifted. They are. Authenticity is an important component of clinical excellence because it frees us to be true to ourselves, which frees us to be true with our clients. Ultimately, it is our culture of grace that allows us to be authentic. We have learned to be real with God (good, bad, and ugly). Therefore, we are able to reflect permission for realness to our clients; liberty is the result of authenticity.

PHIL'S STORY

Let me tell you about Phil. When he first came to me for help, Phil claimed he was struggling with alcohol and cocaine addictions. When we spent time together, I could see clearly how these addictions had taken control of his body. He was always jittery and on edge. However, as our relationship grew, I began to sense that there was another piece of the puzzle that Phil was keeping from me—something other than drinking or drugs. I even felt challenged by God to dig a little deeper into my client's story to see what I might find. So I did.

One day when I was with Phil, I asked him if there was anything else going on in his life that he wanted to discuss. Brushing it aside, he said no and continued to complain about a recent DUI. I couldn't tell exactly what was going on, but

I sensed that Phil was not being authentic. So I pressed him a little more. "Are you sure there isn't something else you want me to know about?" He gazed around my office, fixing his eyes on an old picture on my wall that showed Jesus on the cross. "Are you a Christian?" he asked me. I hesitated for a second, but then I said yes. I assured him I had no intention of forcing my spiritual beliefs on him. "You know," Phil spoke up, "there is something else going on."

From there, I listened to Phil explain how God had called him to do a particular job that he didn't want to do. He felt that God wanted him to encourage and confront Christian ministers who were struggling with hidden problems. Rather than obeying, Phil ran from God and picked up drinking and cocaine. He was afraid of what God had called him to do. After that conversation, Phil and I both knew his deepest issue was his fractured relationship with God, not his addictions.

Several weeks after Phil stopped seeing me, I ran into him again—this time in my own living room! Phil had taken up a job as a cable guy and was assigned an installment at my house. Walking through the door, he recognized me immediately (though reluctantly). We laughed together, but I could sense he wasn't thrilled to see me. He still carried fears and addictions.

Another four years passed. One day, as I was stepping into my beautiful '63 Chevy, I heard a voice yelling from down the street. *"That's him!"* I turned, and to my surprise it was Phil running toward me. We greeted each other with laughter and excitement. "I'm finally doing what God called me to do!" he said. He went on to explain his journey to seminary in New Jersey and, ultimately, to God's purpose for his life. Now, Phil works for a ministry that supports Christian ministers—the very thing he ran from years ago. "And it's all because of you!" he told me.

I love this story because it shows how authenticity impacts others. When I was first seeing Phil, nothing seemed to work. I was frustrated and agitated that we couldn't get to the bottom of his issues. However, when I was able to be authentic and adjust my approach with him, something clicked. He saw that I was being real with him, so he could be real with me. Phil's situation was more complicated than I first understood. It took a broader sense of knowledge to get to the bottom of his problems. But God's grace eventually challenged *both* his fears and his addictions.

NATHAN'S STORY OF GRACE

So what exactly is God's grace anyway? Grace should never be abstract or confusing. It should be clear and active in all our lives. At Stronghold, we understand God's grace as a back-door invitation to His study—an invitation to put your feet up on His table and rest in the den of your loving Father. This gift is based on Jesus Christ's work for us, not ours. It doesn't matter what you have done or what you will do. Grace is God accepting us (knuckleheads) into his own life. All He asks us to do is trust Him.

Once a man named Nathan came to see me. I quickly learned that Nathan did not care to see me himself; he was only in my office because the elders of his church had sent him—he was having an affair. In fact, Nathan confessed to me that he was okay with his affair. When I learned this, I told him I wouldn't help him unless he wanted to see me. I *couldn't* help him until he saw how deadly his affair truly was. So he left. But six months later I saw Nathan's name on my schedule. I knew he must have signed himself up.

When we met, Nathan sat across from me and confessed that the affair had finally gotten to him. His daughter walked in on him having sex with the woman. His affair partner became pregnant and took a serious turn for the worse. His wife found out about the affair and was forcing him to make a decision between her and the other woman. This situation was ugly. Then Nathan looked at me and said, "You were the only person I knew I could talk to about this."

People come back to grace. They don't come back to laws, threats, or judgment. I believe Nathan came back to see me because he knew I would show him grace and be real with him. I could have judged him for wrecking his marriage. I could have just taken his money when his church sent him. I could have been religious or legalistic. But that's not what grace does.

Instead, I offered Nathan safety, consistency, and acceptance. I showed him that my commitment to him as a person was bigger than his mistake. In the same way, people truly go to God when they see how He has loved them through Jesus. Jesus is proof that God's commitment to us is greater than our sins. He isn't waiting for us to clean up our lives before we come to Him. He's just calling us to come as we are—to trust and run to Him—so that He can change us. This is God's grace.

PART TWO

THE STRONGHOLD DIFFERENCE

CHAPTER THREE

DIAGNOSING REALITY

The most painful problem that every one of my clients deals with is sin—a word I don't use lightly or often. Many people understand sin as simply *bad* behavior. With this understanding, we can all *do* sinful things, or we can do good things. However, I believe it's more complicated than that. Sin isn't just the wrong stuff we do; sin is a cage that surrounds and suffocates everyone outside of God's grace. We can still do things that look good when we are actually acting sinfully. It comes in many different flavors and takes on many forms, but sin is always sour and destructive; it forces us into pretense and hypocrisy. Many of our clients struggle to understand themselves truthfully because their sins—or the sins of others—have blinded them from reality, from seeing clearly. So, in this chapter I want to explain one of the most crucial parts of my work at Stronghold: diagnosing reality.

In Jeremiah 2:13, God says, "My people have committed two sins: They have forsaken me, the spring of living water, and have dug their own cisterns, broken cisterns that cannot hold water" (NIV). I think this is a keen depiction of what missing the mark looks like in our lives. Because sin is a power, a principality, and the dynamic that drives law, we forsake God, who is "the spring of living water." Among other things, this means that sin's job is to focus us on performance not connection. As long as we attempt to perform or work our way to God, our poor, inconsistent performance keeps us from accepting His graceful approach to us. We don't want to face Him when under sin's influence.

However, when we turn away from God we also turn away from ourselves. Hypocrisy makes it impossible to face our imperfections and faults. It's just too painful to be honest with ourselves without God—and suddenly we feel very *alone*. I don't know about you, but when I feel alone, I am prone to lean on my own understanding. In fact, solidarity somehow forces us into this trap: when we feel alone, we think we *have* to solve our problems ourselves. Sadly, this lone orientation is the most common denominator in people with serious emotional disturbances, whether they seek help or not.

We have a passion for reconnecting people to themselves. Ironically, clients usually want us to offer them advice for cleaning up their lives. But our first step is helping them see that they are merely created beings, which means they *need* help outside themselves. They need to look into the mirror with a friend who can tell them what they see. So a large part of diagnosing reality in our office is looking into mirrors with clients and telling them how *we* see them—physically, emotionally, spiritually, or otherwise. I think people not only need this but often long for it.

HELPING YOU SEE

I remember the first time I saw Lisa in the hospital. A kind and hesitant woman, she came to me for help with her severe anorexia. Lisa weighed a mere seventy-five pounds—basically starting to blow away in the wind. She once confessed to me, "Everyone keeps telling me I'm skinny, but *I don't see it.*" Lisa's eyes had been blinded by her anorexic tendencies and could not see that her body was very unhealthy. She actually believed she was fat and overweight. So I proposed a challenge to her.

We sat across from one another in the quiet of her hospital room. "You know I can draw," I said to her, tearing a blank sheet of paper in half and handing her one half. She nodded. "I'm going to draw how I see you on my sheet of paper. You draw how you see yourself on yours." Quietly, she complied and began to sketch away. Only a few moments passed before she put her pencil down and held up the paper. On it Lisa had drawn three connected circles that resembled a pig, snout and all. "This is how I see myself," she spoke softly. My heart sank, but I kept drawing.

Once I'd completed my drawing, I handed it to Lisa: it depicted a frail, sickly emaciated woman wearing a hospital gown. "I don't look like that!" she reacted quickly. I looked her in the eyes and responded, "Yes, you do, Lisa. You *know* I can draw. I'm not messing around. This is how you look." Still, Lisa would not believe me. All she saw when she looked in the mirror by herself was Porky Pig. Maybe you can relate?

I knew she needed others to speak truth to her situation, so I instructed Lisa to take both drawings with her and find two different nurses that she trusted, show them the drawings, and ask which one looked more like her. Reluctantly, she agreed. Later, Lisa came back to her hospital room crying. Sitting before me again, she pleaded through her tears, "How come I can't see it? They both said I looked like your drawing. Why can't I see it?"

Tragically, Lisa's story is a common one. Pain and addiction prevent people from looking honestly at themselves because it can be so painful to face reality. When we are lost in a smog of deception, we don't want to see the negative, harmful ripples of our decisions; we just want to remain isolated, to be safe.

But we cannot grow, change, or overcome our challenges unless we first face the darkness of our situations. Until we swallow the bad news, we will never truly hear the good news that there is hope—even if it's not the hope we were looking for. The disconnect between our self-perceptions and true reality is bridged when others look into the mirror with us.

If you feel isolated or unsure about your life, I want you to know that Stronghold exists to help you. We want to not only walk alongside you as you assess circumstances but also to speak healthy, truthful, life-giving words to you. In John 8:32, Jesus spoke these famous words: "Then you will know the truth, and the truth will set you free." I want to help you know the truth about your life. Sometimes the truth can be very hard to swallow, but it is the only way to be *truly* free—free from anorexia, anxiety, addiction, and sin. But first, let's look a little deeper into the things that keep us from being honest.

THE SWORD

Shame. In the Bible, Genesis 3 tells the story of The Fall—how Adam and Eve first disobeyed and sinned against God by eating from the *one* fruit tree He commanded them to stay away from. Before this heinous historical event, Adam and Eve lived in harmony with God, each other, and the rest of creation. The Bible says they lived "naked and unashamed" (Genesis 2:25). However, the first action these two took after their disobedience was to cover up their nakedness with fig leaves. They instantly felt shamed and exposed, so they hid from God. Or ... at least they tried.

Shame keeps us from seeing reality honestly. It makes us feel like there is something very wrong with *ourselves*, so we hide behind our own varieties of fig leaves. This sort of faking it only drives us deeper into lies and deception. Over the years, I have learned that shame isn't always directly connected to something we have done but is often connected to the feeling of being exposed. Thus, people can feel shame at any time, not just when they have made a mistake. Sometimes people feel shame and have no idea why! But the deadliest side of shame is that it *causes more shame*. It pushes us even further into self-deception.

I once had a client named Elliot. Elliot struggled with alcohol addiction. He had to deliver a Drug and Alcohol History to his treatment group. However, he insisted that he couldn't speak in public like that unless he had some alcohol in his system already. I didn't believe him and sent him to the class regardless. This was a poor decision on my part. When it was Elliot's turn, he did the history with near perfection—he killed it! He was honest and confident. "That was great!" I said to him after the class, shaking his hand. Elliot had a glum look on his face. Reaching down into his pocket, he pulled out a half-empty bottle of bourbon. "I told you I couldn't do that unless I had some alcohol," he muttered back.

I believe what motivated Elliot to drink before his test was shame. The shame he felt for struggling with public speaking is what drove him in the direction of drinking before his group meeting. Ironically, the alcohol gave him confidence for the history, but it was also the reason he was there to begin with. The most frightening part of a shamed behavior is that it usually *works*. Elliot drank before his test because he knew it was the only way to get through it. But there is something in this life even more powerful than shame.

YOUR SHIELD FOR SHAME

Love is the antidote for shame. Like an umbrella, it can protect us from the pounding rains of vulnerability and guilt, covering us instead with grace and mercy. Love is an active, living, and heart-penetrating agent with the power to effect lasting change in your life—mentally, physically, emotionally, relationally, and spiritually. Of course, we all long to love and be loved genuinely. But *true* sacrificial love can be hard to come by in our hate-crammed world. This is why Stronghold exists: to impart love to our clients. We all need love.

Clients who cannot see their situations clearly often come to me with hypersensitive emotions raging inside them. When I love them by showing grace and mercy, those emotions are able to settle down, allowing them to think and assess their lives honestly again. When they see that I don't react harshly to their problems, they are able to show themselves grace—even as I expose their negative attitudes and thoughts.

I counseled a woman named Anne years ago. She would tell me stories of how she intentionally gained lots of weight as a young girl so that men would leave her alone. Naturally thin and attractive, she experienced sexual abuse and constant attention from men who wanted to "get with her" until she couldn't bear it anymore. As Anne and I developed a relationship of trust at Stronghold, I noticed she started losing weight. At one point I finally noted aloud how rapidly this seemed to be happening. Anne, rather happy I noticed, explained to me that she no longer needed her "emotional coat" to hide from abusive men and relationships. Because of the confidence Stronghold gave her by showing her love, grace, and mercy, she shed 150 pounds!

As a counselor, I have learned it is very challenging to get people to accept grace. As I mentioned earlier, many clients I meet seem hardwired to fix themselves, by themselves. They long to measure up, to be good enough. Grace, on the other hand, requires people to accept an opinion of themselves that is different from their own. For many, this is a tough task. So, when I diagnose reality with clients, I try to be sensitive and careful—not throwing out big, unbelievable compliments or encouragements. If you struggle with negative self-image, you probably won't believe me when I plainly insist, "No, you're a great person!" That's not being real. Sometimes we need to ingest grace by the spoonful, not by the gallon.

Once again, grace is the answer. When we feel disconnected from ourselves or God, it is grace that assures us of God's love and care for us. It is grace that gives us another chance—not just to fix ourselves but also to be changed alongside the care of others. Certainly, it can be difficult to look in the mirror alone, but Stronghold is here to look *with* you and help you see the truth of your circumstances, no matter how dark they may appear. "Then you will know the truth, and the truth will set you free."

CHAPTER FOUR

HOPE WITHOUT HYPE

One of our favorite phrases at Stronghold is "hope without hype." In the counseling world—not to mention everywhere else—people have many different understandings of hope. It usually implies abstract notions of confidence about the future, promising better, brighter days to come. Hope is a charged word in our culture—but everyone seems to want it! However, at Stronghold we believe true hope is deeper than sunny circumstances. In this chapter, we will step into the storms of suffering and hard times, the places where I believe hope shines brightest.

I want to begin by addressing some of the misconceptions people have about hope. That way, we can see how transformative true hope is. To begin, it seems that people use "hope" and "wish" interchangeably, as though they're synonyms. According to this view, hope is shaky and unpredictable.

So, to be confident means you have to pray that what you want shows up. Then once it does, you're left to figure out how to take it captive, because it may just up and leave. The subtle lie underneath this is that hope can come and go as it chooses. Since we don't always *feel* hopeful, our confidence in God's commitment to us wanes. So many people think hope is temperamental or moody, fading in and out of our lives in different circumstances.

This is the most common misconception of hope I face in my clients. We all want hope (whatever we believe it to be), but we can never keep it around for long—it's like asking a butterfly to sit on your finger for an hour. Yeah right! However, at Stronghold we do *not* believe that hope is based on feelings, circumstances, or our ability to stay positive. Rather, hope is confidence in God—confidence that *He is forever connected to us no matter the circumstances!*

Most of the world understands hope as a rainbow after a storm, something to motivate us when we're down. Or we see it as a carrot dangling out there in front of us, never to be secured. But we believe God gives us hope *in the midst of the storm*, not just afterward. This means we can always have hope—even when we don't feel like we do—because God is always with us.

For Christians, hope is ultimately confidence about our relationship and place with God forever. We believe the simple promise of John 3:16: "For God so loved the world, that he gave his only Son, that whoever believes in him should not perish but have eternal life." Because of Jesus, our final destination is to be with our Father. If we do not have a relational perspective of hope, we become discouraged by the trials and sufferings of this life. We assume we are losers or God has abandoned us, or both. Many people just want "hope" to make their present circumstances smoother. But God's offer of hope does not guarantee blessings and ease in this life; it guarantees something much better: life with Him forever, even through horrible circumstances.

HOPE WITHOUT HYPE

Once Jesus was on a boat with his disciples. They were sailing their way across a small sea when a furious storm picked up on the waters. The waves crashed into the boat with loud, thundering pounds. Cold, fat raindrops fell from the black sky. The winds howled in the disciples' ears as they panicked together, scooping buckets of water out of the boat. Jesus, however, was taking a nap in the stern—just relaxing in the face of the life-threatening storm raging around them. Out of ideas, the disciples ran down and woke him.

The Gospel of Mark tells the story as follows: "But he was in the stern, asleep on the cushion. And they woke him and said to him, 'Teacher, do you not care that we are perishing?' And he awoke and rebuked the wind and said to the sea,

'Peace! Be still!' And the wind ceased, and there was a great calm. He said to them, 'Why are you so afraid? Have you still no faith?'" (Mark 4:38-40). We are sometimes like these disciples. We're slow to trust that God cares for us in the midst of the storm. Doubting he'll come through for us, we lose hope and panic. But what I find so fascinating about this story is the way Jesus challenges his disciples to trust in the midst of their fear, especially when he's still with them. I believe he is reminding them (and us) that true hope is not based in safe circumstances but in God's presence with us.

So what is hope without hype? It's just hope without all the attachments—no promise of prosperity now, no smooth sailin', just confidence that God is with us. Hope without hype is believing that His commitment to us is not based on our feelings, circumstances, or security. It will never change. We can be confident that God is *always* with us because God is secure in Himself. He doesn't *need* us to be strong, trustworthy, or noble. In fact, He doesn't even need us at all. But he *wants* us. That is a much better comfort than sunshine after a storm, isn't it?

THE HEART OF CHANGE

Hoping in God does not somehow clear our lives of struggle. It ultimately points us to our connection with God in the new creation. However, this kind of hope *does* have power to change our present lives if we let it. Hope is much more than lazily waiting around to leave this difficult life behind. Many Christians are guilty of this. But what does it take to let hope change us here and now?

A few years ago a spunky woman named Barb started attending my church. At the time, I was filling in as one of our four pastors. I quickly learned that Barb had a muscle-paralyzing disease and was expecting to die within a few years. She was a precious woman, but she was fading, slowly but surely. One day, Barb approached me after a church service and asked me if I would "walk with her." My heart was heavy: I knew this meant that Barb wanted me to encourage and console her until her death. Saddened by the news but grateful for the opportunity to walk with her, I agreed.

Barb and I began to meet weekly for Bible studies and prayer. I would see her every Sunday morning—sometimes walking, sometimes in her wheelchair. I tried as much as I could to encourage her with God's hope. She seemed to cherish our time together so much. One day Barb called to inform me she could no longer leave her hospital bed to come to church or Bible study. I happily adjusted to bring our Bible studies to her hospital room, but I knew this was bad news; Barb was not getting better. Her disease was slowly taking her life away.

But it could not take her hope away. As I continued to meet with my friend on a regular basis, I saw her hope in God grow. Even as her body was fading away from a horrible disease, her confidence in God blossomed and bloomed beautifully like flowers in spring. Most people lose hope when they walk through difficult times. We avoid suffering and hardship at all cost. Barb, on the other hand, found hardship was her pathway to peace. She was more hopeful on her deathbed than ever before. I remember the day she passed away. Her hospital room smelled like death, but her confidence in God was all she had left, and it was all she needed. Barb died gracefully in hope without hype.

THE HEART OF WHOLENESS

Hope has obvious upshots for people on their deathbed. But what about those of us who still have life to live? How does this hope help us live well now? At Stronghold, we see a connection between hope and *healing*. Many times, what clients need when they come to me is healing, not just hope. We have seen that true hope is perspective grounded in connection with God the Father. Healing, on the other hand, is an experience that allows us to live in a divided place with contentment. It allows us to be okay where we are, even if it's not exactly where we want to be. Healing is the ability to breathe in a tense circumstance. Healing is also the ability to understand that God remains connected to you in victory or defeat, faithful or faithless.

Healing can take place over long stretches of time or in spontaneous, crucial moments. I once witnessed a group of young kids persuade their friend, Dylan, to give up his hidden marijuana stash to me so he couldn't smoke it over the weekend. Both he and his friends knew if he relapsed it would only lead to worse things. I could see Dylan's struggle, but in the end he surprisingly gave his drugs up to me. This was a moment of healing for him—thanks to the care of his friends. We all need healing in those times of tension to help us make the tough decisions, but we also need it *after* we have messed up. Healing allows us to turn toward God before, during, or after our mistakes, not to keep running from Him.

HOPE IN COMMUNITY

Dylan's story is a great example of our common need for relationships. We cannot experience hope and healing in a vacuum. God designed us for fellowship with others and with Him. After lots of prayer with God over the years, I truly believe that we all need at least three types of people in our lives:

1) someone who pours into us,
2) someone whom we pour into, and
3) someone who is just like us.

Isolation is similar to shame. We have already discussed the sharp effects shame can have on us. When we are isolated from the love, encouragement, and correction of others, we will soon begin to feel the weights of shame and guilt. However, with the right people in our lives, we can live with confidence in God's permanent relationship with us. We can know healing is a process, a lifelong one, and there are others like us!

True fellowship requires an agreement between friends. The friends I meet with on a regular basis know what to expect from me and I know what to expect from them. We meet each other's needs and we aren't afraid to be challenging or corrective when the situation calls for it. At Stronghold, I encourage all my employees to also find relationships like these to help them become balanced, community-minded people.

What's the result? A community of therapists who are committed to their clients. Stronghold is more than a counseling center. With all of us believing strongly in the powers of love, grace, and mercy, we strive to be *advocates* for our clients rather than just therapists. Ultimately, this means we are not here just to take your money and talk with you for an hour. We want to use whatever means we have to help you experience hope and healing. I hope you can now see that hope sometimes comes without hype. Sometimes God calls us to press on through the pouring rains and doesn't stop the storm. But, of course, this is when hope means the most anyway.

CHAPTER FIVE

GUIDANCE WITHOUT JUDGMENT

When we first decided to start Stronghold, we entertained a few different names for the practice. Interestingly, all of our ideas had one common thread: this is going to be a safe place where everyone is welcome. In chapter one, I told the story of how Proverbs 18:10 inspired me to finally name the practice Stronghold. But now I want to look deeper into what it means for us to actually *be* a stronghold for clients who need a safe place. I want to show you what *guidance without judgment* looks like in a grace-based counseling center.

I don't ever want my clients to worry about what I think of them. Most people I sit across from in my office already deal with loads of shame, judgment, anxiety, and various sorts of trauma—the last thing they need is a counselor who judges them too. So, I try to make two points very clear with you if you're my client: 1) you can bring your storms and addictions into this room—as we work to make this a place of graceful security; and 2) we want to address *anything* that is keeping you from becoming who you were designed to be. This is what it looks like for Stronghold to be a safe place.

These two points are so important because they communicate to our clients that we are not here to judge them. We are not here to judge *you*. We don't see the people who come to us as burdensome patients who pay our salaries. We love our clients the way they are because God first loved us when we were still His enemies. So, at Stronghold we don't make hard distinctions between rich and poor, black and white, addict and saint, male or female. We want everyone to know they are welcomed. From the inside, Stronghold looks like a lion sitting with a lamb.

Rather than judging them, we exist to be a safe place for our clients who *already* feel judged, marginalized, or lost in their struggles. In this world, such acceptance is somewhat unheard of. We are all used to feeling small or flawed next to the impossible standards the world presents to us. So we know there are many people who long for a practice like Stronghold—where they can experience grace-based guidance without more harsh judgment.

JOYCE'S STORY

Years ago I was counseling a woman named Joyce. Joyce worked as a middle-manager in a large corporate organization. However, she was referred to see me because she was in the middle of a divorce with her husband. And she had already had an affair with another man. Every time Joyce came to see me, I sensed that she felt shame from her affair, but also that she couldn't escape it. Her actual marriage was all but dead, and she didn't know where else to turn. I knew Joyce felt judged everywhere she went.

One day Joyce explained to me in her frustration that she simply did not know what to do with this situation. "My marriage is dead," she told me. "We have been to eighteen therapists and I don't think my husband wants me back. I don't think I want him back either." She stopped for a moment before speaking again. "What am I supposed to do?" she asked.

As usual, I felt that there was more to the story than I could see, so I asked Joyce, "Are you *physically* in this relationship?"

Quickly she objected, insisting she had never had sex with the man of her affair. "It's basically just emotional," she responded hastily.

I did not believe Joyce's affair was purely emotional. People generally don't risk their marriage *and* their reputation for purely emotional affairs. As she and I met regularly for the next few months, I periodically pressed her about her relationship with this man. She continued to insist they had never had sex—until one day.

As I usually did, I asked Joyce, "So, you and this man have still never had sex? Joyce, I'm not here to judge you. I just want to help turn this around."

She paused for a moment, staring at the floor of my office, before letting out a deep sigh. "You know, JC," she said, eyes still fixed on the floor, "I've been lying to you. We have had sex a couple of times." Finally Joyce looked back up at me slowly. Her eyes were swelling with fear—but in an instant she realized I wasn't mad at her. I wasn't judging her.

With a grin on my face, I exclaimed, "Oh, I know you've had sex with him! I haven't believed that lie for a second. But the truth is worth waiting for." She smiled back.

When Joyce finally realized I wasn't there to judge her about her affair, we were able to walk and talk through the situation honestly. I knew that Joyce, as a well-respected Christian woman, had lied to me for so long out of fear of judgment. Her reputation and identity were on the line. How could she confess her marriage was broken and she had slept with another man? Ultimately, grace led her to confess.

Once Joyce learned she was in a safe place, she was able to uncover her lies and face the reality of her mistakes with me.

Judgment has a subtle way of building a wall between where we are and where we truly need to be. Like shame and isolation, it keeps us from coming clean or being honest about the hard things. But when love, grace, and mercy tear that wall down, authenticity and truth can come forward. There is no other way to experience true healing. Of course, a safe place is still sometimes a serious place. It was very difficult for Joyce and I to deal with her affair, but it never would have happened if I had threatened her with judgment.

A SAFE PLACE

Stronghold is committed to being a safe place for everyone. This takes shape in our methods for counseling, but it goes beyond that. Most of my stories in this book so far occurred within the walls of my office in Sioux Falls. However, we have two other counseling practices in South Dakota—one in Spearfish and one in Yankton. It is important to us that each of these locations offer the same consistent experience to anyone who comes to us.

Safety and consistency go hand in hand. In chapter one, I listed consistency as one of Stronghold's guiding principles for how we offer grace-based service. This is why we work hard to ensure the services each location offers are consistent with Stronghold's bigger vision: to be a safe counseling center that dispenses love, grace, and mercy. From the paint color on the walls to the attitude of our receptionists, everything is designed to let clients know what to expect from Stronghold. We understand that people feel most safe in comfortable, familiar environments, so we invested years of time, effort, and money into a counseling practice that is just that. Guidance without judgment goes way beyond the walls of my little office.

The distinction between guiding and judging might seem silly to some, but it makes all the difference to us at Stronghold. Judging and guiding are both forms of *confrontation*. But for me, confrontation is not about pointing out right and wrong; it's about pointing out discrepancy. Confrontation in my office is finding inconsistencies in what my clients put before me—inconsistencies in what they think, what they say, what they do, what they *think* they think, and so forth. So what I am really doing when I guide my clients is finding clarity between the points in the stories they tell me. I'm connecting the dots.

Judgment always comes from a one-up posture. Judgment doesn't just find discrepancies in others. It points out flaws and shortcomings. See the difference? I try to do everything I can to ensure my clients that I am not judging them as I confront them in my office. We want to break down the walls that judgment built so we can be transparent and authentic with each other.

As a male who is six-feet-two, I even have to be mindful of my physical posture toward my clients as I sit across from them. I always bend over in my chair to stay at eye level. Sometimes I will even get out of my chair and sit on the floor as I counsel clients—whatever it takes for them to feel safe and respected. Guidance always comes from a one-down posture.

ONE-DOWN

The best example of someone who lived a one-down lifestyle was Jesus. John 4 tells the well-known story of Jesus and the Samaritan woman at the well: "... Jesus, tired as he was from the journey, sat down by the well. It was about noon. When a Samaritan woman came to draw water, Jesus said to her, 'Will you give me a drink?' (His disciples had gone into the town to buy food.) The Samaritan woman said to him, 'You are a Jew and I am a Samaritan woman. How can you ask me for a drink?' (For Jews do not associate with Samaritans.)" (John 4:6-9 NIV).

Jesus knew it wasn't acceptable for Jewish men to talk to Samaritans—especially Samaritan women—at the time. But that taboo didn't seem to faze him. As the story goes on, Jesus converses with the woman, asking about her life and helping her to see her ultimate need for Him to be her Savior and King. This woman probably expected judgment from Jesus. Instead, he shattered the barrier and showed her compassion.

At Stronghold, we follow Jesus' incredible example of humility and compassion. He never treated anyone with a one-up posture. Jesus chose to identify with the outcasts of his time, not the stiff religious people. Our mission is to offer guidance without judgment to those who need it most. We live in a very harsh, fast-paced, dangerous world. Yet, Stronghold stands in that world as a safe place for anyone to come and find rest.

PART THREE

THE STRONGHOLD PROMISE

CHAPTER SIX

WHAT WE DO HERE

In the counseling world, truth can be very ugly and painful. Buried beneath layers of insecurity, self-deception, or fear, truth often amounts to bad news for many of my clients. But genuine transformative work cannot happen at our practices unless we come face to face with reality. Needless to say, this is a challenging situation for both me and my clients. However, over the years I have learned that grace opens the door for truth in amazing ways—it paves the way for truth to step into the light. In this chapter, I want explore the relationship between grace, truth, and, ultimately, hope.

Especially in the counseling office, I find that *ugly* truths are the things my clients have done to other people while *painful* truths are the horrible things other people have done to them. I can call these "things" truths because they are the events or experiences from the past that have chronic effects on clients. Usually because of shame or fear associated with them, people try to downplay these truths because they are too painful to confront. The reason clients seem to avoid the truth is because it can be very frightening. This means the powers of grace can only take effect by prying open a tomb, so to speak. It's dark and cold, and it smells like death inside. But that's usually where the truth lies.

I have seen grace burst through the hardest of truths for many different clients and in countless ways. Because everyone has a unique story, the ways grace works always look unique. So, I now want to look specifically at how grace and truth intersect in the variety of struggling clients who come to me at Stronghold. I believe we all have something to learn from each of them, but perhaps one will speak especially to you.

ADDICTION

For those struggling with addiction, grace is the door to begin talking about their most basic addictive behaviors. It allows them to tell me the *whole* story of their struggle, not just the palatable parts. Once the whole story is on the table, I can help clients get an honest look at their relationship—always an unhealthy one—with their addiction. Relationships with addictions are always give-and-take relationships: the vice makes you feel better, but it always takes over your life. When I show grace to my clients struggling with addiction, they eventually come to a place where they *want* to leave the addiction behind. From there it becomes a matter of what steps we need to take for that to happen.

MENTAL HEALTH

I have found that most of my clients who struggle with their mental health are hiding from *trauma*. Trauma includes anything from a painful childhood experience to divorce—and everything in between. These clients have a relationship of concealment with the trauma in their life. They hide from their trauma and hide it from others. One tragic example of this is a woman who was raped by an ex-boyfriend years ago. Now married, she struggles to give herself sexually to her husband fully. But the sting of her traumatic memories keep her from talking about it to anyone.

Clients with these mental health issues first need honesty with their trauma. Sometimes this just means realizing that their pain *is* painful. From there I try to help them realize that trauma is just a part of who they are—it's not *who* they are. Some clients tell me they are "addicts." I tell them they are people who struggle with addiction. That's different. As grace allows my clients to redefine their relationship with trauma, they begin to heal and find new, healthier identities.

MARRIAGE AND FAMILY

At Stronghold we practice many of the relationship principles and guidelines of psychology professor emeritus John M. Gottman. Gottman is known for his work in relationship analysis and marriage stability. In practice, this means we are concerned with the *conflict styles* of couples who come to us for help. When we can figure out what exactly is causing conflict in a marriage, we can move forward with practical remedies and grace-based advice.

Many times the conflict styles between couples will become apparent as we are in a session. In these instances, I point out the conflict and see how the couple reacts. This is an instance in which it is vital for me to use grace—to guide without judgment. But these are also the beautiful moments where I get to see couples begin to heal right in my office. Grace leads to truth and truth leads to hope.

GROUP COUNSELING

Counseling with a group has tremendous challenges and rewards. I believe that a group in which people are honest with one another can be far more powerful and grace giving than any single counselor. Group honesty can create an environment of healing and encouragement for broken clients. It has the unique, dynamic ability to uncover the truth. However, groups—especially groups of children—are prone to create division. Without a prominent grace-based leader, groups can become hostile cliques that tend to cover the truth or use it as a weapon.

Still, I fundamentally believe group counseling can be a useful way for people to come to terms with themselves and others in a judgment-free zone. Grace allows group members not only to be honest but also to be gentle and caring toward each other as they grapple through life. Maybe a grace-based group is something you long to be a part of.

PLAY THERAPY AND CHILD COUNSELING

When we counsel children at Stronghold, we often used a method called Play Therapy. This method allows children to play freely in a playroom and make choices without any external influence. They won't get in trouble for pretending to shoot someone with a "hand" gun or for acting out a sexual gesture. As I watch the kids, I read all of their actions as projections. Everything they do communicates something. Ultimately, our aim with Play Therapy is to understand which emotions are associated with what actions for the children.

It is important for playrooms to be judgment-free rooms. In the playroom, we use play as a projection screen to get to know the kids. However, if the kids feel judged or controlled from the outside, they will immediately shut down their playing and prevent us from knowing them. When the kids do play freely, it gives me the opportunity to interpret their actions: What toys do they like? Do they bend the rules? Are they more aggressive on certain days? Ultimately, I want to understand *how* they play. Everything kids do in a nonjudgmental, nondirective playroom is therapeutic, giving me a better understanding of what's going on beneath the surface. This is how we use grace to uncover the truth in the lives of children.

RELATIONSHIP COUNSELING

Stronghold's relationship counseling is geared toward dating couples, single parents, LGBTQ partners, agitated coworkers,

and others who find themselves in uniquely difficult relationships. We still strive to apply grace and truth in relationship
counseling, appreciating that these kinds of relationships
present their own particular challenges.

I have had single mothers come to me needing special
help deciding whether or not they want to keep their unborn
babies. Similarly, I have had single fathers come to me who
simply need help raising their kids alone. These clients don't
want or need me to judge them. They are already in extremely
difficult places and often feel the judgmental effects of taboo
because of it. Instead, I listen patiently to these clients and
guide them in their explorations. In my office, I do not rein-
force the social stereotypes these clients are often crushed by.
God's grace leads me to accept them for who they are as He
has accepted me.

In South Dakota, Stronghold is known for dealing with the
most marginalized people around. Our clientele is not always
upscale. We see broken and stigmatized clients every day—
and we love them. However, this isn't always easy. I still have
to tell my employees often to *find a way* to love their clients,
whatever it takes. I naturally love rebellious, knucklehead
teenagers who flip people off and do drugs. But not all the
other counselors at Stronghold have this instinct. Another
woman who works for me is amazingly gifted at dealing with
sexually abused girls. The same cannot be said for me. At the
end of the day, we find motivation to genuinely care for all

our clients because of God's grace to us. We continue to dispense grace because that's what He does.

LIVING IN THE TENSION

I started this chapter by claiming that truth can be very ugly and painful for some people. Even after everything we have seen in this chapter, that remains an understatement. The reality—the true reality—is that we all live in a broken world. Sin is always crouching at the door. I believe grace and truth can generate hope in hopeless people, but even that doesn't remove all the hard stuff of life. Even after they come to see me, most of my clients find that they must live in the tension.

What do I mean by tension? Tension comes because we all want to keep what we have and get what we want. James 4:1 says, "What causes fights and quarrels among you? Don't they come from your desires that battle within you?" We all have conflicting desires that pull us back and forth between where we are and where we should be. No matter how much healing we experience in this life, that tension will always be tugging at us.

I believe the tensions we face should point us to God; they should remind us of our deepest need: Him. Consequently, this dilemma tells us something about human nature and how we each were designed. But we often try to release the tensions through other means—addictions, unhealthy relationships, fits of anger—to feel content for a short time. But if these feelings are meant to remind us of our need for God, we will never feel ultimately content until we are content with God. If we are satisfied with knowing Him as our Father, we will expect the tug called "tension" and see it as an opportunity to face this life on life's terms—and still know God is God and is there for us. He will be enough for you if you let Him, even in the tightest of times.

CHAPTER SEVEN

OUR PROMISE TO YOU

At Stronghold, we are committed to our clients. Some practices are very pragmatic, with tight structures and rhythms that are meant to produce predictable results in their people. Results are important, of course, but they're not necessarily our passion at Stronghold—our passion is people. Our passion is first and foremost for you. With everything you've read in this book so far in mind, here are the four promises we make to every client. This is our promise to you.

1. TO LISTEN

Our first promise is to listen to you with patience, compassion, and understanding. I am very intentional about this because I have learned that people do not simply want to be listened to; they need to feel heard and understood. Our promise to listen is, of course, a fruit of our passion for our clients. We listen because we care.

A large part of any counselor's job is listening. However, I believe every counselor at Stronghold is an *expert* at listening and empathizing with clients. With years of education, training, and experience, I always have a versatile tool belt of skills at hand. I have learned the dynamics of depression, anxiety, OCD, and other mental illnesses and I understand how each one affects my clients. I want my clients to know that, to a certain degree, I *get* what is going on in their lives—even without having experienced it myself. And I want them to feel comfort from that.

Our promise to listen to our clients is tethered to our convictions about humility. Even as experts in the counseling field, we always come to clients ready to learn and grow with them. Every new client I meet has a unique story with chapters that deserve genuine discussions and attention. No single template or matrix for counseling is enough to adequately address those stories; each one is special. And we will listen closely to them all.

2. TO EARN YOUR TRUST

While we are committed to hearing our clients' stories, we understand that we must first earn the right to hear those stories. As we've discussed in this book, many people resist or refuse talking deeply about their lives. That's understandable! I have heard horribly heartbreaking and painful stories from clients in my office; these can be intensely difficult to talk about. At Stronghold, we want to develop a genuine relationship of trust with each client so he or she feels comfortable at all times in my office.

When clients begin to realize they can trust me, they allow me to walk with them through the "behind the scenes" of their distress. In the last chapter I explained how grace opens the door to truth. That principle still applies here, but in a slightly different way: now, clients show *me* grace by letting me into the truth of their lives to help them. I do not believe I have any right to hear the stories of my clients, but I am here to listen.

When meeting new clients, I give time to reading and interpreting what kind of relationship he or she *wants* to have with me. In my experience, each case calls for a different solution. Some clients need intensity and hard questions from me, while others trust me more as I keep calm and listen to them. Many of the older men that I counsel *need* me to pry into their lives before they feel as though they can trust me. Otherwise, they will simply write me off as a softie who can't deal with their messy problems. On the other hand, younger clients tend to seek calmness and stability from me. In either case, I do everything I can to meet my clients' needs and gain their trust without force or coercion.

3. TO PROVIDE THE HIGHEST LEVEL OF QUALITY

Our vision at Stronghold is to be the best. We pursue clinical excellence in all areas of service because we believe you deserve it. So, our third promise is to be excellent, consistent, and effective in whatever ways we can. Each day we ask ourselves, "How can we do better than we did yesterday?" Being the best doesn't require an arrogant *better than* posture toward everyone else. It only means we recognize that we are good at what we do.

When you are very good at something, you don't have to be insecure or judgmental toward others who might be better. True talent allows you enough security to be wrong at times. At Stronghold, you will find a team of confident, trained, compassionate counselors who are eager to dispense love, grace, and mercy into your unique story. Just as God loves in His security and sufficiency, we love our clients out of security and a passion to see their lives heal. We exist primarily to bless and support others—not to abuse or take advantage of their time or money.

I believe one of the most important aspects of our pursuit of excellence is our *humanity*. Many of the counselors at Stronghold (myself included) come from fractured, pain-filled backgrounds, just like many of our clients. In this way we are able to empathize with our clients on profound levels as they begin to tell us their stories. We do not downplay our humanity for the sake of professionalism. Rather, counselors at Stronghold respectfully embrace the human commonalities we have with our clients to serve them better without judgment. As a team, we represent a wide range of challenging life experiences. These experiences have molded us into a dynamic, talented, passionate group of counselors who are committed to excellent grace-based counseling.

4. TO BE A REFUGE

Lastly, Stronghold always promises to be a refuge to those who are hurting. Based on Christlike love, grace, and mercy, we eagerly welcome all people regardless of culture or creed. We are a safe place for anyone to come and deal with their addictions and ailments. However, we are *not* a hiding place. Just because clients feel safe here does not mean they always feel comfortable.

As we have seen, uncovering truth from the cellars of our souls can be a painful business. But that's what Stronghold is all about. So, while we are a refuge for the broken, we are simultaneously a place where people experience the discomfort of facing reality. Though this can feel like gazing into an endless, ominous void, by God's grace this is how we grow and heal. Stronghold wants to look into the mirror with you.

By now you know I'm crazy about God's grace. Grace has reoriented the way I understand the counseling office, but also the world beyond. Stronghold does not exist only for Christians but for anyone who needs a safe space to rest and grow—Muslims, Buddhists, those of Native tribes, Atheists, and others. As an African American man in Sioux Falls, South Dakota, I especially identify with and fight for minorities. I understand how strenuous it can be to find a refuge when you feel marginalized and suffocated by society. But I don't care who you are or where you come from, Stronghold stands for you. There is always more grace.

These are our four promises to you. We promise to listen, to earn your trust, to provide clinical excellence, and to be a refuge for you as long as you need. My aim with this book is not to gain more clients but to help more people get their lives back together. If you're wondering whether or not Stronghold is a place for you, let me say this: You are not reading this book by accident. I believe God is always working in our lives. Is He asking you to do something? To finally have that conversation? To leave that toxic relationship? Maybe He's even asking you to visit Stronghold.

God rarely calls us to do things alone. He has given us the precious gifts of one another. So, if you're feeling compelled to make a change in your life, or to obey His calling, do it with someone who knows Him already. If you want to come see us at Stronghold, bring a friend. No matter how far gone you may feel today, Stronghold can be a refuge for you. I hope this book has proven to you that God's love, grace, and mercy are never exhausted. No one is too lost to be found by the Great Shepherd. Even now He calls out to each one of us: "Come to me, all who labor and are heavy laden, and I will give you rest" (Matthew 11:28).

CONCLUSION: EXPERIENCING THE STRONGHOLD DIFFERENCE

As I began this book, I told you the story of how Stronghold started with one question: Is a counseling center that is characterized by *both* clinical excellence *and* grace possible? I hope the answer to that question is abundantly clear to you by now—*Yes! It is possible!* Through years of refinement and growth, Stronghold has become such a place. We have worked hard to cultivate a safe space saturated in God's love, grace, and mercy for those hurting around us. And we work hard every day to ensure it stays that way.

I also began this book with an invitation to grace, and I want to end where I began. That invitation is not hypothetical or rhetorical—it's a literal invitation for *you* to step out of judgment and into a new world where grace has the last say. But you may be wondering *How do I accept such an invitation?* Let me offer you some guidance about how to take the next step forward.

PROSPECTIVE CLIENTS

If you are a prospective client who has not yet contacted Stronghold or any other counseling service, my first advice is to visit our website at www.strongholdcounseling.com and decide if Stronghold is a place you can see yourself. By clicking the "Staff" tab, you can see and read about all of the therapists who work at Stronghold. From there, you can choose a therapist who seems right for you and call our office to set up an appointment: 605-334-7713.

If you don't think Stronghold is the right place for you, I urge you to find someone else who can help you. Find a pastor, teacher, family member, or mentor who can meet with you regularly, listen to you, and offer you grace-based guidance—someone who knows God and can help you know Him more. Accept the invitation to grace!

CURRENT PATIENTS

If you are a current client at Stronghold, I hope this book gave you some "ah ha!" moments. Hopefully you have a better understanding of why we do what we do at the practice. I have given you a look behind the curtain of our operations. My desire is that these chapters have given you a deeper appreciation for the things we do at Stronghold and the people who work here. Maybe you have found a new perspective on what brought you here in the first place. Most of all, though, I hope you feel how extremely loved you are by Stronghold. Continue on in your dance with grace!

STAFF AND INTERNS

I hope this book gives my staff and interns a better look into my heart for them. Stronghold is ultimately a place that *we* have co-created. I could not have done this alone. Because of you all, we are constantly refining and becoming better each day. For that I am so grateful.

I hope this book helps you understand that I am remarkably proud of you. The excellent grace-based work you each do every day is what keeps this ship afloat and sailing toward brighter, better days. I pray you continue that work with me— by the grace God provides you. From a shepherd's perspective, I guess you could say I've got a damn good flock.

PROSPECTIVE PARTNERS

Lastly, if you are a prospective partner reading this, I want to thank you for showing interest in Stronghold. I also hope this books gives you a keener sense about *what* we do and *why* we do it. As you have learned, Stronghold is a unique counseling center. As such, it requires particular kinds of people and standards to maintain its day-to-day operations. We joyfully welcome partners into our practices; however, we do expect all partners to meet our standards and needs. Once you are in the "loop," we will support and encourage you all we can, but we are committed (as you have read) to consistency from first to last at Stronghold. It is a central part of our work in reaching and helping the broken in our communities. Please visit our website for further information.

"May the grace of the Lord Jesus Christ, and the love of God, and the fellowship of the Holy Spirit be with you all" (2 Corinthians 13:14 NIV).

ABOUT THE AUTHOR

DR. JAMIE "JC" CHAMBERS

I would like to take this opportunity to introduce myself as one of the founders at Stronghold Counseling Services, Inc., as of January 1994. I am a transplant to Siouxland, as I am originally from Denver, Colorado, but found my way here by way of central Kansas.

I received my bachelor's degree in art and education in 1983 from Sterling College in Sterling, Kansas. I moved on from there to receive my master's degree in counseling from North American Baptist Seminary here in Sioux Falls, South Dakota, in 1985. Immediately following the completion of my master's program, I applied and entered the doctoral program at the University of South Dakota at Vermillion, completing my doctorate in counselor education with an emphasis in family therapy in 1992.

I am a licensed psychologist, marriage, and family therapist, and professional counselor in the state of South Dakota. I am a clinical member of the American Association of Marriage and Family Therapists and I have been an AAMFT Approved Supervisor since 2001. I have been trained in Adlerian Individual Psychology throughout both my master's and doctoral studies. This approach is very helpful when examining the impact of family life on life-style decisions. I am also trained as a licensed addiction counselor and since 1985 have worked extensively with adolescents and adults who are dealing with chemical dependency issues. I am also a Master Life Space Crisis Intervention trainer and a Senior Response Ability Pathways trainer.

I can provide quality family, group, couples, individual, and play therapy services. I have been trained to assist people in addressing the following issues: chemical dependency and codependent family living, abuse issues, marriage issues, parent/child and parent/teen conflicts, disordered eating issues, trauma therapy, spiritual abuse issues, and most recently, trained in the use of dialectical behavioral therapy, and offer clinical supervision and program management.

2 Corinthians 1:3-4 states: "Praise be to the God and Father of our Lord Jesus Christ, the Father of compassion and the God of all comfort, who comforts us in all our troubles,

so that we can comfort those in any trouble with the comfort we ourselves have received from God" (NIV).

As stated above, graceful living is the organizing theme of my practice. I believe God enables me to assist others in the enterprise of living life on life's terms. We need to learn how to honestly and mercifully confront the problems of life in a manner that minimizes avoidance and defensiveness, and maximizes responsible relating and problem solving.

I am also available for community outreach services, seminars, public information, and education services. Hope can be restored through experiencing God's grace, love, and mercy.

Contact Dr. Chambers

Website: StrongholdCounseling.com
Email: info@strongholdcounseling.com
Phone: (605) 334-7713
Fax: (605) 334-5348
Address: 4300 S Louise Ave, Suite 201
Sioux Falls, SD 57106

ABOUT STRONGHOLD COUNSELING SERVICES

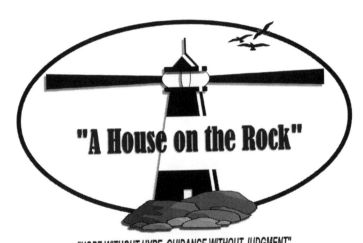

"A House on the Rock"

"HOPE WITHOUT HYPE, GUIDANCE WITHOUT JUDGMENT"

STRONGHOLD COUNSELING SERVICES

OUR MISSION

The name of the Lord is a strong tower; the righteous man runs into it and is safe. – Proverbs 18:10 (NIV)

Stronghold started as a vision of founding partners JC Chambers, Ed.D., and Marlene Ruff, M.A., as a place where those who are hurting could experience both clinical excellence and God's grace. There are certainly many fine treatment centers specializing in traditional clinical care along with several outstanding Christian-based counseling services. However, we find the combination of these two healing approaches to be unique.

The mission of Stronghold is to dispense God's grace in reaching those outside the church door while providing services that are clinically astute, sound, and at the highest level of excellence. Stronghold is not in the business of preaching, judging, or proselytizing. Stronghold is about healing. The kind of deep healing that happens when therapy resides on the spiritual level, addressing all the elements that make up the whole person.

THE STRONGHOLD DIFFERENCE

Stronghold was created in 1993 to offer Hope, the hope of real healing for those hurting in a broken world. Healing never takes place alone. Many times it is the result of deliberate, intentional, caring service from committed professionals with years of experience, professional counselors who have already helped hundreds in similar situations. This hope is the foundation of the Stronghold experience.

HOPE WITHOUT HYPE

Healing is never easy. There is no quick fix. It is often painful. It does not happen overnight. But real, life-changing healing can and does happen regardless of what often may seem like a mountain of overwhelming circumstances. True, we don't know what you're going through. But at Stronghold, you'll never have to face it alone.

GUIDANCE WITHOUT JUDGMENT

Stronghold was founded on a philosophy of nonjudgmental counseling. Before healing can happen, open communication must take place in a safe environment free of judgment. Stronghold provides a "judgment-free" zone where individuals and families can honestly open up, often for the first time without any fear of repercussions.

Contact Stronghold

Website: StrongholdCounseling.com

Email: info@strongholdcounseling.com

Phone: (605) 334-7713

Fax: (605) 334-5348

Address: 4300 S Louise Ave, Suite 201

Sioux Falls, SD 57106